P9-CKS-891

MEMOIRS OF A GEISHA
A PORTRAIT OF THE FILM

Introductions by ROB MARSHALL
and ARTHUR GOLDEN

Photographs by DAVID JAMES

Text by PEGGY MULLOY

NEWMARKET PRESS

Memoirs of a Geisha, the film: TM & © 2005 Columbia Pictures Industries, Inc. and DreamWorks L.L.C. and Spyglass Entertainment Group, LLC. All rights reserved.

All rights reserved. This book may not be reproduced, in whole or in part, in any form, without written permission. Inquiries should be addressed to Permissions Department, Newmarket Press, 18 East 48th Street, New York, NY 10017.

This book is published in the United States of America.

First Edition

10 9 8 7 6 5 4 3 2 1
1-55704-683-2 (Hardcover)

10 9 8 7 6 5 4 3 2 1
1-55704-694-8 (Paperback)

Library of Congress Cataloging-in-Publication Data available upon request.

Book cover on page 9 from *Memoirs of a Geisha*, by Arthur Golden. Reprinted by permission of Vintage Books, a Division of Random House Inc.

QUANTITY PURCHASES
Companies, professional groups, clubs, and other organizations may qualify for special terms when ordering quantities of this title. For information, write Special Sales Department, Newmarket Press, 18 East 48th Street, NY, NY 10017; call (212) 832-3575; fax (212) 832-3629; or e-mail info@newmarketpress.com.

www.newmarketpress.com

EDITED BY LINDA SUNSHINE   DESIGN BY TIMOTHY SHANER

Manufactured in the United States of America.

OTHER NEWMARKET PICTORIAL MOVIEBOOKS INCLUDE:
Kingdom of Heaven: The Ridley Scott Film and the History Behind the Story
Ray: A Tribute to the Movie, the Music, and the Man
Vanity Fair: Bringing Thackeray's Timeless Novel to the Screen
Two Brothers: A Fable on Film and How It Was Told
Schindler's List: Images of the Steven Spielberg Film
Cold Mountain: The Journey from Book to Film
In America: A Portrait of the Film
Saving Private Ryan: The Men, The Mission, The Movie
The Art of X2: The Collector's Edition
The Art of X2: The Making of the Blockbuster Film
Amistad: A Celebration of the Film by Steven Spielberg
Chicago: From Stage to Screen—The Movie and Illustrated Lyrics
Catch Me If You Can: The Film and the Filmmakers
Frida: Bringing Frida Kahlo's Life and Art to Film
E.T. The Extra-Terrestrial: From Concept to Classic

Contents

I guess I've always been in love with movies that take me away from the everyday and transport me to an unknown world. The films of David Lean, for example, are always able to do that on a grand scale. *Doctor Zhivago, Ryan's Daughter, Summertime,* and *A Passage to India* all give you a passport to an exotic place and time, allowing you to believe that for a few hours you are somehow a part of it all. Movies can do that. I believe that's what, in part, led me to *Memoirs of a Geisha.*

After the singular experience working on the film version of Kander and Ebb's *Chicago,* I was looking for a challenge of another sort. My hope was to find some-

OPPOSITE: Director of photography Dion Beebe, camera operator Peter Rosenfeld, director Rob Marshall and Ziyi Zhang. RIGHT: Rob Marshall, Ziyi Zhang and Ken Watanabe.

thing completely different, where I could immerse myself entirely in another genre. Then along came a call from our renowned producers Lucy Fisher, Doug Wick and Steven Spielberg. They asked the intriguing, yet intimidating question: Would I bring Arthur Golden's glorious novel to the screen? The answer was an excited (albeit nervous) "Yes!"

Geisha's story appealed to me because it not only peers into the fascinating and forbidden world of a geisha's life in 1930s Japan, but also tells the emotional tale of one particular girl's journey. A journey that, like the water seen in our heroine's blue-grey eyes, continues to forge its own path even when met with adversity and hopelessness. This I found deeply moving.

I began my own journey by meeting with the mastermind behind all of this, Arthur Golden. He answered questions from the silly to the profound and helped me unlock the intricacies of

INTRODUCTION

Sayuri's Journey

BY ROB MARSHALL

Sayuri's life. A more open and collaborative artist you will not find.

I then began assembling my "team." I was fortunate to get the majority of the creative force that had worked with me on *Chicago*: cinematographer Dion Beebe, production designer John Myhre, costume designer Colleen Atwood, stills photographer David James, hair designer Lyn Quiyou, lead cameraman Peter Rosenfeld, associate choreographer Denise Faye, development assistant Arthur Roses and, of course, my invaluable lifetime collaborator and right arm John DeLuca. This time John would not only choreograph and direct second unit as he had before, but would also serve brilliantly as the film's co-producer.

Added to this extraordinary team was yet another stellar group: executive producers Patty Whitcher and Bobby Cohen, casting director Francine Maisler, Japanese casting consultant and interpreter Yoko Narahashi, geisha expert Liza Dalby, make-up designer Noriko Watanabe, dialect coach Jessica Drake, assistant director Eric Heffron, script supervisor Lyn McKissick, master writers Doug Wright and Robin Swicord, visionary editor Pietro Scalia and legendary composer John Williams.

Every step we took together was challenging, thrilling, frightening and rewarding. From time spent in Kyoto and Tokyo researching this uniquely mysterious culture to the many weeks in rehearsal rooms applying everything we'd learned, each layer, like a beautiful kimono, revealed yet another layer.

When it came time for casting, I had the insane desire (as most directors do) to work with the greatest actors in the world. Who knew that with *Geisha* that dream would actually be realized? The all-star international cast is awe-inspiring to say the least. In short, they are: the incandescent Ziyi

Zhang as Sayuri, the elegant Ken Watanabe as the Chairman, the breathtaking Gong Li as Hatsumomo, the exquisite Michelle Yeoh as Mameha, the great Koji Yakusho as Nobu, the delicious Youki Kudoh as Pumpkin and the divine Kaori Momoi as Mother. Rounding out the cast are the wonderful actors Tsai Chin, Cary Tagawa, Randall Duk Kim, Eugenia Yuan, Mako, Kenneth Tsang, Togo Igawa, Thomas Ikeda, Ted Levine, Samantha Futerman, Zoe Weizenbaum and the amazing Suzuka Ogho as young Chiyo. With five of my principal actors making their English language debut, rehearsal and filming were intense. I have to say, however, that the amount of hard work and dedication that I witnessed was overwhelming. And even though one would think that directing actors through interpreters would be an impossibility, eventually it became not only familiar, but

truly a non-issue. I found that another language was created between us. An intimate language that naturally exists between director and actor no matter what barriers there are.

Now that we are almost finished (I am currently in the last weeks of post-production), to say that I am honored and humbled to have been a part of this beautifully shared experience is truly an understatement. Hopefully we've done some justice to this magnificent and alluring fable. Perhaps we've even been able to transport you to that place we all yearn to go—somewhere beyond the everyday that magically exists, then simply disappears, leaving us wanting more.

LEFT: Sayuri (Ziyi Zhang) practices shamisen. RIGHT: Sayuri lets go of her dreams.

INTRODUCTION

Through a Painter's Eye

BY ARTHUR GOLDEN

What is it like to have a novel turned into a movie? The only way of answering that question is to begin with what it's like to write a novel in the first place. I've always believed it's one of the most complicated things you could ever do with your mind. The sculptor Henry Moore once said, "The secret of life is to have a task, something you devote your entire life to, something you bring everything to, every minute of the day for the rest of your life. And the most important thing is, it must be something you cannot possibly do." That would be writing a novel.

After you've begun with the simple problem of writing prose, you have to add to it the challenge of managing the story itself, while at the same time thinking of the historical and cultural possibilities and also imagining the inner lives of the characters. It's like driving in fog on a crowded road while reading a map and troubleshooting a serious problem with your car. When it's over you can only roll down the windows and wipe your forehead. What's left behind some time later is the memory that you put just about everything you had into a struggle and somehow made it through. But just barely.

In certain ways I can hardly remember writing *Memoirs of a Geisha* at all, in spite of the many years I spent doing it. I do remember one moment when I had index cards all over the floor of my study as I wrestled with a problem of the story's construction. I also remember a moment during a weeklong visit to my mother's house when I realized that an approach I'd taken to a scene with Mameha wasn't going to work. The only thing I remember throughout, from beginning to end, was the feeling of struggling with an enormous beast that seemed always on the brink of outwitting me. Every time I felt a sense of relief at finding my way through some difficult passage, a new set of problems came along.

In the years since the book came out, I haven't reread it or been tempted to. That feeling of taking a hazardous drive on a foggy road is still too much in the front of my mind. So perhaps you can imagine how curious it was for me to walk around a full-scale geisha district of the 1930s, built on a field in Ventura, California, and know that such an enormously detailed movie set grew out of something that involved tearing up index cards in frustration, and deleting long passages that had taken me weeks to write, and most of all, counting words again and again to see whether I could stop for the day. Sometimes the cast and crew members asked me if the things I'd seen during filming looked the way I'd imagined they would, and I had to answer that they didn't, not at all—though I hurried to add that I wasn't disappointed, and in fact quite the

opposite. I was amazed. Here in front of me was something far too fully realized to have grown out of those murky images in my head. While writing the book I wasn't using the medium of stunning visual imagery but of language, and language is a poor vehicle for rendering the real world with any precision. (If you doubt this, just go read a police description of a suspect, or the set of instructions for assembling a toy.) Like any writer, I had to make do with creating the *illusion* of a scene, evoking a summer day by means of beads of perspiration on a forehead, or an untidy room by means of the stain on a tatami mat. I was certainly never required to imagine whether a character's hand in a certain scene might be resting on her knee or in her lap, or whether a teacup lifted from the table a

OPPOSITE: Ziyi Zhang, author Arthur Golden, and Ken Watanabe on set. RIGHT: Arthur Golden's best-selling novel.

moment earlier had left a ring there—though of course, in making a film, precisely these sorts of questions must indeed be settled.

Maybe that's one reason why as I've watched this movie come together, I've often had the feeling of a man who has gone to sit in a room beside a painter with a canvas, and then after closing his eyes and describing a scene, has opened

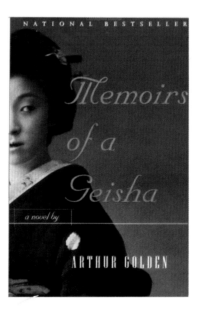

them again to find a complete and beautiful painting of it. I am deeply moved, not by the scene as I've described it in words—a scene which has after all existed in my mind for quite some time already. Rather, I am moved by the painter's remarkable achievement. And I don't mean just the resplendently gorgeous actresses in their perfect kimono, or the atmospheric lighting, or the simple drama of a character shown walking through a doorway. It is, rather, the remarkable experience of standing on a chaotic soundstage, with women wearing headsets, and men with clipboards and walkie-talkies, and watching everyone suddenly freeze when the signal is given. And now the camera closes in on the actresses, while nearby stands the painter himself, Rob Marshall, wearing his headset and watching his monitor, somehow understanding how every one of these many brush strokes will come together seamlessly to make the painting. ▨

Like the image of Sayuri on the spring festival dance poster, geisha can seem more mythical than real, as if they belong to the realm of legends, mirages and dreams. But they are flesh and blood women, completely unique to Japan, with a history that has frequently been misunderstood.

A geisha is first and foremost an artist—the word *gei* (pronounced gay) means "art" in Japanese. For centuries, geisha have emerged from their homes at dusk, like butterflies from cocoons, to begin that night's round of teahouse engagements. Over the years, they have come to embody traditional Japanese culture with their dances, songs and musicianship. Just as embedded in geisha identity is their place in the world of powerful men.

Their roots wind back to Japan's isolationist Edo period, which began in 1600. During this long era of hierarchical shogun rule, licensed pleasure quarters were established, which allowed the government to regulate and tax prostitution.

The courtesans who lived and worked within these strictly drawn districts were flamboyant figures who fascinated the public. Dressed in towering clogs and many layers of elaborate kimonos, they rarely stepped outside the licensed quarters. Artists immortalized them in woodblock prints, and admirers collected their pictures. Nightlife revolved around parties where they held court with wealthy patrons and members of "the floating world"—actors, artists and others outside respectable society whose style defined the era.

Geisha were invited into "the floating world" in the early 1700s. The very first geisha were actually men who played traditional drums and told amusing stories. The first woman appeared around 1750, and by 1800, the profession was definitively female. As the novelty of courtesans faded, geisha replaced them in the public's imagination as style icons. Like courtesans, geisha were often associated with Kabuki actors in gossip and in private life.

But geisha were entertainers, not women of pleasure, and their appearance emphasized this. Their obis were tied in back, not in front like courtesans', and their kimonos, hair and make-up were

OPPOSITE: Set decoration poster from the film. RIGHT: Archival image of apprentice geisha circa 1910.

The Life of Geisha
Does She Really Exist?

much more subdued. Because the rules of the pleasure quarters prohibited geisha from engaging in the courtesans' business, it was important to make the difference clear. When legalized prostitution ended in 1957, geisha carried on as usual because they had never been prostitutes.

Nor have they ever been wives. Although geisha spend many hours entertaining and catering to men, they belong to a world that is run by women. Instead of children and a home, they dedicate themselves to art. Geisha who decide to marry leave this world behind. Falling in love with married men is a risk they take and the subject of some very sad geisha songs.

Geisha may not have always chosen their own destinies, but the days when desperately poor families sold their children have long passed. Women who become geisha today are often drawn to the profession through an interest in the traditional arts and may remain in it only a few years. In the past, the role tended to last a lifetime, and was even passed along from mother to daughter.

Hana is Japanese for "flower," and the geisha life has long been known as "the flower and willow world." The *hanamachi* or geisha district belongs to women during the day. The *okiya* or geisha households have been here for hundreds of years, along with the vendors and service businesses that cater to the geishas' needs. As night falls, it becomes a man's world.

A social evening has traditionally been an important part of conducting business in Japan, and the presence of geisha reflects well on the host who can afford the luxury of these glamorous com-

LEFT: Archival Japanese postcard.
RIGHT: This pair of two-fold silk screens by Ikeda Terukata shows an intermission at a Kabuki theater, circa 1915.
Courtesy of Fukutomi Taro Collection.

panions. With wives typically excluded from such evenings, geisha add a different kind of feminine presence. They keep the atmosphere convivial and the sake cups full, and show just the right amount of embarrassment when the humor turns raunchy.

That a geisha is discreet is an absolute given. She learns many secrets as business is conducted and sake is poured, which closes her world to all but a trusted few. Political coups have been plotted on *tatami* mats. The overthrow of shogun forces, which ended the Edo period and restored the Meiji emperor in 1868, was strategized in a Gion teahouse.

Teahouse talk is not all business, but a witty, well-informed geisha remains in demand after her beauty fades. In guiding Sayuri, Mameha stressed that becoming a deft conversationalist would be one of her most important skills if she hoped to attract a *danna*, or patron.

A *danna* enjoys an intimate rela-

tionship with a geisha and underwrites her expenses. Although Mameha emphasized a geisha's need for lively intelligence in securing such an arrangement, she also understood the role of fantasy and desire in attracting a wealthy patron. She schooled Sayuri accordingly: "You cannot call yourself a true geisha until you can stop a man in his tracks, with a single look."

A geisha's style of dress and behavior may strike Westerners as modest, but for many Japanese, its very subtlety is arousing. What is hidden and what is suggested have always been part of the geisha's allure.

Until the middle of the 20th century, a geisha's first sexual experience or *mizuage* was a commodity brokered by the mother of her *okiya*. The money paid by the man who deflowered her helped pay some of her debt to the *okiya* for living expenses, lessons, kimonos and other trappings of

her lifestyle. After *mizuage*, she was a *maiko* ("apprentice geisha") no more, and the red collar under her kimono was replaced by a full geisha's white collar.

The geisha's role as fashion trendsetter began to fade as Western influence became equated with modern in Japan. After World War II, the number of women who undertook this disciplined life fell dramatically. During the post-war occupation, some women who

called themselves geisha traded sexual favors for money. Soldiers knew them as "gee-sha" girls.

As in many professions, standards have always varied within the geisha world. Not all geisha have aspired to the level of artistry that top geisha pursue, nor have all been as selective about sexual partners. The atmosphere at resorts where "hot springs geisha" make their living, for example, is nothing like an exclusive teahouse.

The geisha districts described so vividly in Arthur Golden's novel still exist today, and authentic geisha continue to entertain in elegant old teahouses. They dress, groom themselves and perform as geisha have for centuries, although they are more likely to arrive at engagements in a client's luxury sedan than a rickshaw.

The man who chooses to entertain honored guests in this setting has committed to an expensive evening, but there is nothing else like it in the world today. ◙

Ageisha's training has always emphasized the arts that define her: dancing, traditional Japanese singing and playing music. (Most identified with the three-stringed *shamisen*, the geisha also studies the flute and drums.)

For many years, a girl who was a prospective geisha began her lessons as a small child, sometimes as young as three, and this life decision was rarely hers. If a close relative was a geisha or a teahouse owner, the "flower and willow world" was a natural path for the child. A poor rural girl who had been taken into an *okiya* as a servant could also be sent to geisha school if the *okāsan* (mother of the household) saw potential in the child. The *okāsan* kept careful track of the cost of her lessons and other expenses, expecting to be repaid when the girl matured.

Today's geisha start their studies later, and of their own accord. Schools are located in each geisha district in a community building

You are to become a geisha

that also houses the geisha registry office and the theater where the annual seasonal dances are held. Lessons in tea ceremony and calligraphy are also part of the training.

A girl's success has always required not just commitment to her lessons, but the ability to learn from what she observes in the *okiya*, watching the senior geisha. As she helps the geisha dress for their evening rounds, she is also learning proper etiquette and demeanor.

Before the war, a girl would graduate from the cotton kimonos of a child to the spectacular silks of a *maiko* around the age of 11. Now a new *maiko* is more likely to be 16 or 17.

In essence, a *maiko* is a peacock. Her vibrant make-up, elaborate hairstyles, colorful kimonos and resplendent obis indicate that she

is on the brink of blooming. A *maiko*'s older sister is the geisha who orchestrates her debut and introduces her at the teahouses. The sister pact is formalized at a private teahouse ceremony where the *maiko* takes a new name, often derived from the older sister's.

The *maiko*'s life is hectic as she continues her studies, performs at the public dances and attends evening social engagements with her older sister, cultivating one of the most important of the geisha's arts, good conversation. After four or five years as a *maiko*, she is ready to "turn the collar"— exchange her red *maiko* collar for a geisha's white one—and take her place as a full geisha. 🔳

RIGHT: Archival image of an okāsan *(mother of the household), right, and* maiko *(apprentice geisha).*

PORTRAIT OF THE FILM

For I have lived my life again, telling it to you.

MAKING *MEMOIRS*

Arthur Golden's *Memoirs of a Geisha* was embraced by critics and public alike upon its release in 1997, and spent two years on *The New York Times* best-seller list. It has sold more than four million copies in English, and has been translated into 32 languages. Its popularity also fed an appetite for a screen adaptation.

Set in a mysterious and exotic world that still casts a potent spell today, the story begins in the years before World War II when a Japanese child is torn from her penniless family to work as a servant in a geisha house. Despite a treacherous rival who nearly breaks her spirit, the girl blossoms into the legendary geisha Sayuri. Beautiful and accomplished, Sayuri captivates the most powerful men of her day, but is haunted by her secret love for the one man who is out of her reach.

Director Rob Marshall was among the many who savored the entrée that Golden's novel provided into the hidden world of geisha. But he was equally drawn to the universality of the young orphan Chiyo's plight and her eventual triumph after an accidental meeting changes the course of her life. "This story lives in a very specific world, and yet the underlying theme of the triumph of the human spirit against all odds connects to any culture," said Marshall. "The fact that this one child, after being taken from her home and sold into slavery, can survive and ultimately find love affected me profoundly."

The story's themes of hope and survival inspired producers Doug

RIGHT: Darek Gogol's concept illustration of the cherry blossom viewing party.

Wick and Lucy Fisher, partners in Red Wagon Entertainment, in their seven-year quest to bring *Memoirs of a Geisha* to the screen. "It was a triumphant character in a strange and wondrous world," said Wick, "and we knew it belonged on the big screen."

Wick, the Academy Award®–winning producer of *Gladiator*, acquired the rights to Golden's novel soon after it was published, and gave a copy to Sony Pictures Chairman Amy Pascal (then president of production). Fisher was the vice chairman of the studio at the time. "I couldn't put the book down," she recalled. "It was as if I had been given a passport to another world I never wanted to leave. I couldn't wait to see the movie."

Fisher had a strong hunch that Steven Spielberg would also fall under

Overview

Striking a Flint for Luck

the novel's spell, and she was right. He signed on as director, and preliminary pre-production work began.

"Culturally, it was one of the most fascinating stories I had ever encountered," said Spielberg. "I was also very moved by the love story, by the rivalry between Sayuri and Hatsumomo, and by the test of friendship between the Chairman and Nobu. I thought it was relevant to people in every country. It was certainly relevant to me."

However, after several near-starts, it became clear that Spielberg's calendar could not accommodate the demanding project. He bowed out as director but remained on board as a producer. *Memoirs of a Geisha* attracted many suitors over the next few years, but never the right one.

Then Fisher saw an advance screening of *Chicago*, and knew

RIGHT: Rob Marshall welcomes key cast and crew at the start of "geisha boot camp." Visual props include a scale model of the hanamachi.

she had found her director. "Rob Marshall knows how to make everything the most accessible, the most dramatic. We pursued him ardently, but he didn't return our calls for many months. He was busy opening *Chicago*."

That film, a boldly modern telling of a tale from another era and Marshall's feature film debut, was a critical and commercial sensation recognized with a string of top awards including the Oscar® for Best Picture and five additional Academy Awards®. Marshall had many options after the Oscars® in 2003, but the question he heard most was, "Which musical would you like to do?" Musicals were not on his wish list. "I wanted to do something completely different, to step into another world."

Suspecting that might be the case, Wick and Fisher bided their time—and were rewarded for their patience. "When we finally sat down with Rob and he told us his vision of the movie, it was exhilarating," said Wick. "He had absolute clarity about his path through the novel. We could almost see the movie when he talked about it."

Meanwhile, Arthur Golden, at home in Boston, sometimes wondered if the movie would ever be made. "My daughter was the first one in our family to see *Chicago*," he recalled. "She came home and said, 'Dad, this movie was made for you.' I went the next night and was madly in love with it. It was a better version of the play that I had loved. So when I heard that Rob Marshall was interested in directing the movie of my novel, I was thrilled."

When Marshall came on board, he thought it was important to find a woman writer and Robin Swicord was brought on to write a new draft of the script. Pulitzer Prize-winning playwright Doug Wright later joined the team and polished the shooting script.

Marshall reunited key members of his *Chicago* behind-the-camera unit, beginning with his Oscar®-nominated director of photography, Dion Beebe. Production designer John Myhre and costume

RIGHT: Producer Doug Wick, Sony Pictures Chairman Amy Pascal, Rob Marshall, executive producer Patty Whitcher, producer Lucy Fisher and executive producer Bobby Cohen at the film's Los Angeles-area hanamachi *set.*

designer Colleen Atwood, both Oscar® winners for *Chicago*, also joined the production, while John DeLuca returned to choreograph and co-produce.

Two important behind-the-scenes artists who were new to Marshall also joined the team. Editor Pietro Scalia, an Oscar® winner for *Black Hawk Down* and *JFK*, had worked with Wick on *Gladiator*, and was now invited to edit *Memoirs of a Geisha*. Creating music to underscore the drama of Sayuri's journey was another huge undertaking and the filmmakers were thrilled when John Williams, a frequent Spielberg collaborator and five-time Oscar® winner, agreed to compose the score.

On the business side, Gary Barber and Roger Birnbaum, co-chairmen of SpyGlass Entertainment, were intrigued by the project. With long-standing ties to the Japanese film market, they offered to co-finance, which took *Memoirs of a Geisha* over its last hurdle to a full production green light.

In pre-pre-production mode, Marshall and his team had been vigorously researching their subject. "We had decided to tell

Sayuri's story as an impression of a time and place, but needed to understand the reality first," said Marshall. "We all agreed that total immersion in Sayuri's world was the only way to begin, so we traveled to Kyoto together to experience everything we could. We built a collective set of memories and references on this trip that we drew from constantly in the months that followed."

Memoirs of a Geisha begins around 1930, near the end of the geishas' golden era. While the novel is set in Kyoto's Gion *hanamachi* or geisha district, the film is set in an unnamed *hanamachi* in Miyako, which is Japanese for "capital."

The group of 10—Marshall, DeLuca, Fisher, Swicord, Beebe, Myhre, Atwood, executive producers Patty Whitcher and Bobby Cohen, and assistant Arthur Roses—explored the novel's terrain. They visited museums and shrines, toured a kimono factory, attended a sumo match, rode in rickshaws, scouted the coast of the Sea of Japan, watched a *maiko* make-up and dress, saw the spring festival dances, attended a Kabuki performance, and were entertained by geisha at the exclusive Ichiriki Teahouse (the film's elite teahouse is called Yukimoto). Marshall also met with actors in Japan. He cast five lead roles—the Chairman, Nobu, Pumpkin, Mother and Chiyo—with

Japanese actors, four of them stars and one a young novice.

After a worldwide search, Ziyi Zhang (*House of Flying Daggers*) won the title role as Sayuri. Oscar® nominee Ken Watanabe (*The Last Samurai*) was cast as the Chairman. Michelle Yeoh (*Crouching Tiger, Hidden Dragon*) plays her mentor, Mameha, and Gong Li (*Raise the Red Lantern*) portrays her bitter rival, Hatsumomo. Koji Yakusho (*Shall We Dance?*) plays the Chairman's business partner, Nobu. Youki Kudoh (*Snow Falling On Cedars*) plays her childhood friend, Pumpkin, and Kaori Momoi (*Kagemusha*) portrays Mother. Suzuka Ohgo, who recently made her movie debut in Japan opposite Watanabe, plays Chiyo, the child who becomes the geisha Sayuri.

The cast arrived in Los Angeles for intensive rehearsals well before production began. Geisha boot camp, as it was called, included dialect classes, scene rehearsals,

OPPOSITE: An altar at Yoshiminetera in Kyoto. RIGHT: Rob Marshall and Suzuka Ohgo.

dance classes, costume lessons and sessions with Liza Dalby, the production's geisha consultant. A cultural anthropologist, author and former geisha herself, she helped the actresses learn the subtleties of geisha demeanor and body language. She also coached them on playing the three-stringed *shamisen*.

Marshall took the cast through every word of the script during rehearsals, with Doug Wright making adjustments for language as they worked. "Rob could always find the emotional essence he wanted," said Fisher.

Kaori Momoi, a veteran of more than 40 films, felt changed by working with Marshall. "Rob-san is such a strong and clear-cut director that, for the first time, I just accepted whatever the director said. I never saw him angry. I can-

not believe such a director exists. I myself tried to be a little more gentle."

Michelle Yeoh had a similar feeling. "Rob has two sides: silk and iron. He gave us the time and space to be our most creative, but always kept a clear vision of what he wanted us to do."

Principal photography began Wednesday, September 29, 2004, on Stage 14 at the Sony Pictures Culver City lot and wrapped Saturday, January 29, 2005, under a rainy sky in the Shizuoka prefecture of Japan. Most of the film was shot in California, three months in Los Angeles and two weeks in

Northern California. The final work was done in Japan at ancient shrines, temples and monasteries, primarily around Kyoto.

The very first scenes were shot inside Nitta *okiya*, the fictional geisha household where much of the story takes place (Nitta is the family name). Young Chiyo (Suzuka Ohgo), frightened and exhausted, has been dropped at the doorstep like an unwanted parcel. As Auntie (Tsai Chin) leads her through the house to be sized up by Mother (Kaori Momoi) and Granny (Kotoko Kawamura), Chiyo's new life, far from home and loved ones, begins.

Although Ken Watanabe was not scheduled to work that first day, he was on set for the official start of production. With everyone gathered in a circle, he offered an invocation in Japanese to notify the heavens that this group was committed to creating something great. He then lead the group in three rounds of three claps each—a custom called *sanbonjime*—to make it official. ❧

Cast

Ziyi Zhang as
SAYURI

Ken Watanabe as
THE CHAIRMAN

Michelle Yeoh as
MAMEHA

Gong Li as
HATSUMOMO

Koji Yakusho as
NOBU

Youki Kudoh as
PUMPKIN

Kaori Momoi as
MOTHER

Suzuka Ohgo as
CHIYO

In his novel *Memoirs of a Geisha*, Arthur Golden painted a portrait of a mysterious and hidden Japanese world. "Arthur's descriptions and observations were intoxicating and impossible to forget," said Rob Marshall. "From Tipsy House to teahouse, the details were so intimate and so immediate that Sayuri's surroundings seemed to breathe. As a filmmaker, I was in awe of his ability to create such an intensely visual experience."

Marshall knew that bringing this textured atmosphere to the screen would be a colossal challenge. He entrusted the building of that world to John Myhre, his Academy Award®-winning production designer on *Chicago*. Myhre loved the novel and was eager to visit the places Golden had so vividly

OPPOSITE: Darek Gogol's early concept illustration of the hanamachi *set. RIGHT: Production designer John Myhre.*

described. "Arthur shared some of his research notes with me and I used them as my guide," he said.

Dion Beebe, Marshall's Oscar®-nominated cinematographer on *Chicago*, was enlisted to photograph *Memoirs of a Geisha*.

"Backlot" *hanamachi*

While scouting in Japan, Marshall, Beebe, Myhre and executive producer Patty Whitcher quickly saw obstacles to filming in a real *hanamachi*. "Even in the beautiful ancient cities, we could not find an area of businesses that was untouched by modern elements and that we could control for as long as we needed," Marshall explained.

"Control" meant changing seasons on a day's notice. "One day we might need 24-foot trees with cherry blossoms, two days later those trees had to be green, and two days after that, bare and

covered with snow," said Myhre. "We needed the equivalent of an old-fashioned backlot."

A backlot *hanamachi* would require a huge piece of property for its dozens of buildings, curving maze-like streets, bridges and river.

The film's other location needs included hot springs, Japanese gardens, a Sea of Japan and a palatial Baron's estate. After scouting trips on several continents, a plan emerged: to shoot most of the movie in Los Angeles with an

Production Design
A Hidden World

additional month of location work in northern California and Japan. Most interiors would be shot on soundstages at Sony Pictures Studios in Culver City. The film's *hanamachi* district would be built at Ventura Farms, a sprawling horse ranch about an hour outside L.A. with mountains in the distance and 360° green valley views.

With a plan in place, Myhre started playing with tiny foam-core models of two- and three-story *hanamachi* buildings. He laid them out on a desktop at a meeting with Marshall one day. "Three hours later, we had a floor plan that we stayed with through the entire film," said the director.

Next came a full set of technical drawings for 40 buildings, and then a quarter-inch model with toy cars and rickshaws, tiny people and the carved path of a serpen-

tine river. The model provided a frame of reference for early decisions, from planning the construction budget to choosing the film's format. "It was rushed to meetings in the back of [art director] Tomas Voth's car many times," Myhre laughed. "We put a little lipstick camera inside the model and could view on a monitor what it was like to be in there. Dion and Rob played with it all the time and even used it to plan a complicated crane move for the first winter scene."

Beebe confirmed: "It was a great way to walk through the possibilities of the *hanamachi* set before it completely took shape."

Magic hour all night long

The sun is bright out at Ventura Farms, which was lovely for the film's spring and summer scenes, but would pose huge problems when the story

called for flat winter light. "I was ushered into the art department to see the model," recalled key grip Scott Robinson, "and the first question everybody asked was, 'How do we make this look like wintertime?' I looked at Dion and our gaffer John Buckley, and we all instinctively knew we had to silk it in."

Altering light by filtering it through a "silk" is a common technique but covering this enormous set with a retractable silent grid cloth—a.k.a. silk—was a very bold idea. "Patty Whitcher told me failure was not an option," said Robinson, "because once they chose southern California as their location, she knew this had to be done."

Robinson's Rags 'n' Rigs crew created the largest freestanding structure ever built over a set,

LEFT: Scale model of the hanamachi *set. OPPOSITE: "Silking" the* hanamachi *set for a winter scene.*

covering nearly two acres. At Marshall's command, rigging grips unfurled 1.75 acres of sailcloth—actually six separate panels or "rags"—across Kevlar lines suspended between two trusses. The 450-pound rags could subdue light by day, or keep out the dark at night. The trusses that supported them resembled lighting towers at a giant outdoor concert. Anchored by tanks holding a million gallons of water and held together with 10,000 bolts, they spanned 250 feet and were tall enough to accommodate 60-foot Condor lights.

"A lot of thought went into the logistics and engineering," said Beebe. "We knew that wind would be an issue out there, and noise, with so much flapping material above us. We only got it done because a lot of brave people took a chance. It contributed immensely to the look of the film."

The silk also allowed filmmakers to shoot night for day. Gaffer

Buckley could contain and control light under the silk no matter how black the sky beyond the set perimeter. "We had magic hour all night long," said Whitcher, referring to the fleeting soft light at the end of the day.

Maybe too much sometimes. "I think," said Beebe, "we all had those moments at three in the morning when we were shooting a day scene, and then would step out into the black void and remember, oh, it's nighttime."

Designing around the action

The transformation of the Ventura Farms location from horse pasture to *hanamachi* was completed in 14 weeks with about 175 crew members contributing. "This is the largest town I've ever built," said construction coordinator John Hoskins. "It was rolling hills and weeds when we got here. We brought in heavy equipment and graded a 400 foot by 400 foot pad, then cut a river through the

center of town." About 250 feet long, 22 feet across and eight feet deep, the river—an important visual symbol of Sayuri's nature—had a re-circulating system that created the illusion of running water.

The river also added geography—

ABOVE : Shooting night for day at the hanamachi *set. OPPOSITE ABOVE: "Beautiful Little Bridge" at the* hanamachi *set. OPPOSITE BELOW: The Japanese Pavilion at Golden Gate Park.*

window and laughed when I went inside and saw that it was in a pot!" said the author. "The attention to detail was awe-inspiring. You couldn't tell that it wasn't a real village or a real river with real moss and real trees."

The set was built with cedar, bamboo and clear fir. Black bamboo and sheets of cedar bark, both unavailable in the United States, were shipped from Japan, along

with fences made of woven grass and bamboo. Set decorator Gretchen Rau, a veteran of *The Last Samurai*, bought huge quantities of window coverings, reeds and mats for the *hanamachi* while shopping in Kyoto. Her shopping spree yielded five big containers of set decor. In addition to visiting dealers, warehouses and Kyoto's version of Home Depot, she made sure to spend two Sundays in the

buildings could be north or south of it, or on Main Street. "We marked the whole town out on the ground with stakes and strings so we could walk through it," said Myhre. "Then we acted out the scenes so that we could design around the action. We also started naming things to keep it all straight: Okiya Street, Crab Alley, Mameha Lane, Beautiful Little Bridge, Slab Bridge, Car Bridge."

Many architectural details came from photographs Marshall, Beebe and Myhre had taken in Japan. "Some pictures are whole buildings," said Myhre, "others just a keyhole, or the end of a roof, or a plant growing through a wall."

That last detail delighted Golden when he visited the set— his first visit to any film set. "I was admiring a beautiful Japanese-style juniper tree protruding through a

city to shop the temple markets. "It gives heart to whatever you're doing when you bring real things to the set," Rau said.

The structural surfaces of the *hanamachi* were sandblasted to add texture and age, then stained, rather than painted. Roof tiles, all separately sculpted and molded, were modeled after pieces purchased in Japan, as were *shoji* screens. The streets were stamped concrete, lending more subtle texture. And when the shooting schedule called for seasonal shifts—so important in Japanese culture—greens foreman Danny Ondrejko was ready with four hand-made cherry trees for each time of year. Outgoing trees were carried away by crane and stored until their season returned. Later,

The pre-war hanamachi *set.* OPPOSITE: *By day, with Michelle Yeoh, Ziyi Zhang and boom operator David Roberts.* RIGHT: *By night.*

some spring boughs—with every blossom applied by hand—were used again in San Francisco and Japan.

The *hanamachi* challenged and delighted the cast and crew. "This set was very important to me," said Ken Watanabe, "because my character first meets little Chiyo here, on the bridge, and that meeting changes the course of her life—and the Chairman's. I worried about that scene, and the idea that my character could have such power over someone, but this beautiful set helped make it real for me."

Golden saw the *hanamachi* set as an idealized geisha district. "When I was writing, I did everything I could to re-create the real Gion on the page," he said. "But Rob fictionalized it as 'a geisha district,' which gave him freedom to focus on the things that were most important to the story he told."

The *hanamachi* was bulldozed after the film wrapped. "It was sad

to let it go," said Marshall, "but this was a beautiful valley when we arrived, and it has returned to that. The horses have their pasture back and we have our *hanamachi* on film."

Looking through the veil

Most buildings at the *hanamachi* set were only exteriors, but several had fully executed interiors on soundstages. These included the Nitta *okiya*, the Yukimoto teahouse, Dr. Crab's clinic, the public baths and Mameha's apartment.

The two-story *okiya* was designed to look about 150 years old. Much of Sayuri's story unfolds in its rooms—from her arrival as Chiyo on her first night in the city to the explosive fight between Hatsumomo and Sayuri years later. The *okiya* aged considerably more after that fight and the subsequent fire.

"All of the *okiya* was a delight—the intricacy of the architecture, its beautiful linear aspect—you can develop characters in these interiors," said set decorator Rau, who furnished the rooms. "Rob understands the importance of patina on things, especially in a world where everything is so old."

Cinematographer Beebe enjoyed the opportunity to explore the

story's contrast between electricity and oil lamps, and the tension it reflected between the modern world and the older ritualized *okiya* and teahouse ways. "Rob loves a faded, aged aesthetic, an almost tobacco-stained world of

ABOVE: Ken Watanabe, Rob Marshall and Dion Beebe.

118

layers and textures," he said. "We lit a lot of things in the *okiya* from oil lamps and flame. Those warm, flickering light sources added mystery and depth."

The world outside the *okiya* was filmed in a variety of locations, many in California. Muir Beach, on a rugged stretch of northern California coast, portrayed the Sea of Japan, while the Tipsy House clung to a cliff overlooking Moss

Beach, a few miles away. The outdoor hot springs at Descanso Gardens near Pasadena were ideal for the post-war resort scenes; the resort interiors were filmed at

ABOVE LEFT: The Fujimi Inari Shrine near Kyoto. ABOVE RIGHT: Early concept illustration of Tipsy House. BELOW RIGHT: The Tipsy House set overlooking Moss Beach, California.

Hakone Gardens in Saratoga, about an hour from San Francisco.

The Baron's estate was filmed in four locations. He hosted his lavish blossom-viewing party at Huntington Gardens in Pasadena, where a special cherry tree was hand-carried onto the set in six-foot sections (the Huntington did not allow truck or helicopter deliveries in the area). The Baron's exterior was some distance away, at a hundred-year-old mansion in Tokyo. The long entrance to his "lair" was created at Yamashiro Restaurant in the Hollywood Hills, and the gold-leaf lair itself was built onstage at Sony. Yamashiro, originally modeled after a house in Kyoto, also provided locations for the geisha school and the exterior and courtyard of the Kaburenjo Theater.

Memoirs of a Geisha also filmed inside the Japanese Pavilion in San Francisco's Golden Gate Park. Sayuri and the Chairman had an important emotional scene in its garden. Mameha, Chiyo and young Pumpkin are also seen here, as are the boughs from the cherry trees.

The *Geisha* filming unit in Japan was tiny: 16 people from the U.S. crew and about 36 Japanese counterparts. The Americans arrived in Kyoto on a Friday night and spent the entire next day scouting with the Japanese crew. Filming began just after dawn on Monday in a frosty bamboo forest on the outskirts of Kyoto.

The next day, *Memoirs of a Geisha* had the good fortune to be one of the rare foreign films invited to film at Kiyomizutera, a Buddhist temple on stilts in Kyoto. The temple was founded in 778 and rebuilt in 1633. "We felt so honored to be there," said Marshall. "We arrived before dawn to shoot the sunrise and it was magical—silent, majestic, like a dream."

The production filmed at several other temples, shrines and monasteries in Japan, including the Shinto Fujimi Inari Shrine near Kyoto, a visual inspiration for Christo's "The Gates," which became the talk of New York the following month.

The last shot of the production was filmed in Japan's Shizuoka prefecture. The crew traveled for 90 minutes on a bullet train and another 90 minutes on a chartered bus through hilly tea-growing terrain to reach the banks of the Ohi River. The star of that day's work was a huge vintage steam engine as it crossed (and recrossed) an old bridge. Modern and ancient Japan intersected once again.

"We've chosen to shoot *Memoirs of a Geisha* in a way that makes you feel like you're looking through a veil," said Beebe. "You peer into a world that you hadn't seen before and you weren't necessarily supposed to see, but here you are."

LEFT: Kiyomizutera in Kyoto.

LEFT: Extras dressed for a post-war hanamachi *scene.* OPPOSITE: *The* hanamachi *set dressed for war.*

A 1200-year-old city and Japan's imperial capital for more than 1,000 years, Kyoto is a place of rare beauty, rich history and cherished traditions. With annual festivals as ancient as its temples and shrines, the city has long been a cultural and spiritual center. Although spared the carpet-bombing that leveled much of Japan, Kyoto was immensely changed by World War II.

In the film, the city is called Miyako, which means "capital." To distress the beautiful *hanamachi* set for wartime, production designer John Myhre began by shuttering shops and businesses and removing many of the signature red lanterns from the streets. "It was no longer prospering, people were lining up for rations, but it was still Japanese," Myhre said.

The Japanese Army occupied the city then, and eventually forced the evacuation of the *hanamachi*. To remove its pre-war luster, Myhre had the entire set sprayed with gray and sand-colored paint. He coated the streets with a special loose sand that produced clouds of billowing smoke as vehicles plowed through. A way of life was disappearing in the dust.

The American post-war occupation, from 1945 until 1952, altered the *hanamachi* again. "It became Americanized and took on a completely different look and feel," said Myhre. "We washed down the streets on set and aged the buildings a bit more. All the businesses changed."

Businesses that had thrived for generations tried on new identities. The sake shop promised whiskey; the noodle bar advertised hamburgers, and the doll and fan shop was selling cheap tourist goods. "G.I.s Welcome" was widely proclaimed.

Myhre looked to photographs of the era for inspiration and information about the signage that

Kilroy was here

blanketed the city. "The signs were horrible, black and white, on wood or scrap metal, big block letters, mostly misspelled," he said. "They were put up to pull the Americans in. They were the opposite of before [the war] when everything was simple, beautiful and unassuming."

Ugly vending machines leaned against the exclusive Yukimoto teahouse. Another teahouse became a coffee shop, its *tatami* mats replaced by cheap tables and chairs for the Americans. The few lanterns that survived were shabby and torn, and the dogs in the streets were underfed. Half of the female extras in postwar *hanamachi* scenes were playing prostitutes.

"It all looked torn and frayed and unsettled," Myhre sighed. "It was very sad, but that is what we were trying to achieve." 🏮

A geisha has a mission when she dresses for the evening—to present herself as living, breathing, Japanese art. Wearing a kimono is a commitment to elegance, best mastered by studying Japanese dance.

Costume designer Colleen Atwood was eager to immerse herself in this world of nuance, and to collaborate once again with director Rob Marshall after winning an Oscar® for her work on *Chicago*.

Creating drop-dead gorgeous kimonos for stunning actresses like Ziyi Zhang, Gong Li, Michelle Yeoh and Youki Kudoh was one part of the designer's job. In addition, there were hundreds of other characters to outfit including peasants in a fishing village, denizens of the thriving *hanamachi*, aristocratic party guests in Western fin-

OPPOSITE: Costumer Jay Cheng adjusts an extra's obi. RIGHT: Costume designer Colleen Atwood.

ery, Japanese soldiers and desperate evacuees, the post-war *hanamachi* population and wealthy New Yorkers of the 1950s. "It seemed that almost every day we shot a huge scene that was different than the day before," Atwood said. "I designed the whole movie up front and knew what I wanted for every costume by the time we started shooting. But I was still making costumes until the end."

Wearing kimono well

"The thirties were a high point of the geisha world so these women had a lot of kimonos," said Atwood. "They were very into fashion and many designed their own in collaboration with kimono makers. The *okiyas* also commissioned them as investments, which their geisha wore but did not own. Wealthy patrons commissioned them as gifts for their favorite geisha.

"A kimono is a fairly simple garment—just eight yards of fabric—but what creates value are all the layers of technique involved," she explained. "A really high-end one would have hand-painting and *shibori*, a very specific dyeing

technique, as well as hand-embroidery and a hand-woven, hand-designed obi. Each element involves a huge expense and huge amount of time. It takes about a year to make one in Japan."

A geisha chooses her kimono

Costume Design
Like an Artist Needs Ink

and obi to match the season in color, weight and visual motif. She wears a two-piece undergarment of red silk next to her skin, then a slip and a cotton top with a collar—red for *maiko* and white for geisha. It dips low in back to reveal the nape of the neck, a highly erotic part of the body in Japanese culture. She also wears an under-robe which is glimpsed when she walks and sometimes peeks below the kimono's hemline.

Wrapped as tightly as a corset, the obi holds the kimono in place and supports the back during long hours of sitting on the floor at the teahouse. *Maiko* wear a long red silk scarf underneath the obi, wrapped around the body 10 times to thicken the waist and create a straight line.

"We took some liberties on that point with our glamorous actresses," Atwood allowed. "What we have is much, much simpler than what they do in Japan. We had to make things lighter and easier to get on and off."

The *Memoirs of a Geisha* actresses developed their own signature kimono style by rehearsing in them every day for almost a month before filming began. Daily dance classes helped them cultivate geisha body language.

"Wearing kimono every day was quite beautiful for me because it is my own culture," said Youki Kudoh, who plays Pumpkin. "It helped me understand how we became Japanese. You cannot move like you're wearing jeans. You learn to be elegant. You reconstruct yourself as a woman. It is very sensual."

It was inspiring for Atwood, too. "The art of kimono could be a lifetime endeavor," she said, "and in that context, I barely got to scratch the surface. It is an art

LEFT: Costume illustration for one of Hatsumomo's many kimonos. OPPOSITE (clockwise from top left): Three illustrations for Sayuri's kimonos, illustration of Mameha's "plum blossom" kimono.

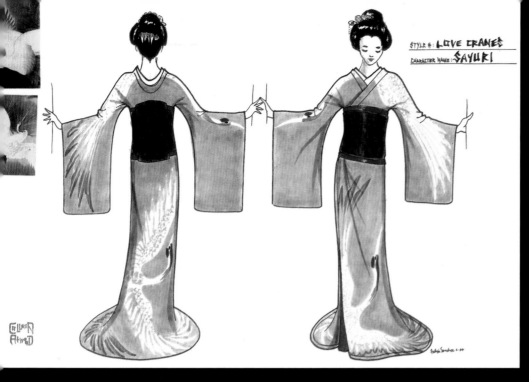

STYLE #: LOVE CRANES
CHARACTER NAME: SAYURI

STYLE #: PLUM BLOSSOM BR
CHARACTER NAME: MAMEHA

form when all the elements, including movement, reach a certain aesthetic level. The look recurs in the cycles of Western fashion because it is so special and beautiful. I think the low neckline in back will definitely be noted by the fashion world again soon."

A bygone world

Rob Marshall chose to tell Sayuri's story as an impression of a bygone world, and wanted the look of the principal characters to have a feeling of fable. "Sayuri is sharing her youthful memories with us, the most dramatic episodes of her life," said the director. "We wanted our lead characters to look the way Sayuri saw them—larger than life."

A dazzling example of this vision is the recalcitrant diva, Hatsumomo, played by Gong Li. Always a dangerous presence for

Sayuri, Hatsumomo wore much stronger colors and patterns than a real geisha would. Even her sleeve-length defied regulations. "Hatsumomo is a fashion character," said Atwood, "which to me means a person who doesn't wear fashion, but creates it. She wore kimono with a huge amount of attitude and style."

Sayuri is a child when she first glimpses the Chairman, played by Ken Watanabe. From that moment on, he was her hero. "He was young then so we made him a very tailored, somewhat shiny navy blue suit," said Atwood. "We wanted him to look like a fairy tale person to little Chiyo, and his look remained heroic throughout the film."

Sayuri's life journey was often

LEFT: Hatsumomo (Gong Li) strikes a pose. OPPOSITE: Mameha (Michelle Yeoh), right, teaches Sayuri (Ziyi Zhang) geisha demeanor.

ABOVE: A specialist in the Yuzen style of kimono painting at work in Kyoto's Nishijin district, long famous for kimono making. OPPOSITE: Maiko Sayuri (Ziyi Zhang) and geisha Mameha (Michelle Yeoh).

with a waterfall design that flowed from the obi to the hem."

The liberties taken in designing for the principal characters did not apply to the hundreds of smaller characters and background players. "It was very important to us to know what was real in the time and place we were examining," Atwood emphasized. "I went to the archives at the Fashion Institute in Tokyo and saw great journalism from the period, gritty images that were incredibly helpful."

Kimonos for many background characters were rented from the Yuya Collection in Kyoto, which specializes in Japan's Taisho (1912-1926) and Showa (1926-1990) periods. Other vendors were found in England, Denmark, New York and Los Angeles. "I bought beautiful antique kimonos from a Russian collector on eBay," Atwood said.

She bought many pairs of men's and women's *geta,* or wooden sandals, in Japan. The

likened to the flow of a river and her affinity for water was a constant visual presence in the film. "There were water aspects in almost all of her kimonos," Atwood said. "The best one was at the end, a transparent blue-grey

principal geishas' shoes were based on antique Japanese dance shoes found at the Ikeda collection in Tokyo and custom-made in Atwood's workshop.

She commissioned several items for the film in Japan. "The textiles of Japan are the equal of anywhere in the world. I worked with Tatsu-mura Textile, a 500-year-old company, on an obi that I designed and it was such a satisfying experience. Their style of collaboration and knowledge of the art of weaving were fascinating."

Colleen's shop

Atwood's department made more than 250 hand-finished costumes with a key crew of about 30 people at her Culver City workshop. The crew grew to 50 when the largest scenes were being prepped and filmed. Her shop had women's and men's departments, a textile department, a specialty costume area and a fitting room outfitted with *tatami* mats. Kimonos were made for characters of every socio-economic level, and for every season. Among many other things, the women's department also made costumes for the dance sequences and romantic 1930s cocktail dresses for the Baron's blossom-viewing party. They produced geisha underwear, Pumpkin's glamorous post-war bras and the geisha's white cotton *tabi* socks, which fasten on the side and separate the big toe.

The Western suits worn by the leading men were custom-made by the tailors of the men's department, as were the military uniforms of the General and his aides. The banana fiber skirts the village men wore as they pulled fish from the sea were also created in the workshop.

Key specialty costumer Deborah Ambrosino created several memorable items including the eight-

inch–high lacquered black sandals for Sayuri's dance solo and the hair ornament that became a weapon when Hatsumomo and Sayuri fought.

An on-site crew of textile artists headed by Matt Reitsma handled many projects. Their screening techniques allowed Atwood to replicate and embellish designs from antique fabrics on new material. The fabrics they created included the print used for the robes worn at the hot springs. One of their proudest accomplishments was the dyeing, stenciling, hand-painting and embroidering of Sayuri's blue-grey waterfall kimono.

In his novel, Arthur Golden provided evocative and expert detail about the beautiful kimonos his characters wore, but he never tried to make one. When Golden saw the level of work going on in Atwood's workshop, he joked, "If I had had any idea, I would have put them all in blue jeans."

LEFT: Hair designer Lyndell Quiyou works on a maiko *look.* OPPOSITE: *Inside the hair trailer.*

Make-up

"When a geisha wakes up in the morning, she is just like any other woman," Arthur Golden wrote in his novel. "Only when she sits before her mirror to apply her makeup… does she become a geisha."

A geisha's make-up techniques have been handed down over the centuries. The white make-up known as *oshiroi*, which Kabuki actors wear onstage, is worn by full geisha only for the most formal occasions; a *maiko* wears it whenever she appears in public.

Noriko Watanabe, the film's Japanese-born make-up designer, is an expert with *oshiroi*. "Its texture and consistency are different from foundations we normally use for film," she explained. "It dries fast and will streak if you don't work quickly."

With some filming days calling for 150 extras, Watanabe needed skilled day-players, in addition to her key team so she hosted workshops in Los Angeles before pre-production. "In the course of six weeks, we trained more than 100 people including about 65 high-level union technicians," she said.

Watanabe followed the principles of geisha make-up, but softened some aspects of the look and exaggerated others to heighten the impact of the principal characters' beauty. "To be geisha, they had to be chosen," she explained. "To be chosen, they had to be so beautiful and intelligent that they almost seemed untouchable."

Watanabe and her team followed the traditional process with *oshiroi*: rub a sticky oil called *bintsuke* between the palms and smooth it onto the face, neck, upper back and hands to create a uniform surface. Then apply the white foundation with a wide, flat goat's-hair brush. Follow with a light dusting of powder to set the make-up and achieve a bisque porcelain finish.

When applying *oshiroi*, geisha and *maiko* accentuate the neck's seductive appeal by leaving two V-shaped peaks of bare skin at the nape—three for special occasions. "We painted them a little longer for the film," said Watanabe.

The stark white face flushes as color is added to the lips, cheeks and corners of the eyes. The vivid red mouth is usually painted into an upturned pout, smaller than the actual lips. "The upper side of the cheek is always painted pink for *maiko* to show the innocence," said Watanabe. "Ziyi had fun wearing the *maiko* make-up, which made her look like a cherry blossom herself."

Beauty is cruelty

Hair

A geisha's upswept hair is another trademark and its upkeep is entrusted to a handful of hairdressers and wigmakers in the *hanamachi*. She never wears her hair down in public, unless she is performing a stage role at a public dance. Instead, it is snugly wrapped under a cap and wig. The wig is fashioned into the elegant, subdued *shimada* style, which dates back to the 1790s.

The typical five years of geisha apprenticeship are marked by variations on the split peach hairstyle with a bun in back divided by a strand of red fabric. The hair is adorned with combs, artificial flowers and other ornaments in keeping with the *maiko*'s doll-like appearance.

After steeping herself in historical books, prints and paintings, hair designer Lyndell Quiyou subtly updated classic geisha and *maiko* hair. "Rob said, think of

geisha on a Paris runway, and that's what we did," she explained. "We made the shapes and silhouettes more modern and geometric."

Quiyou and her team spent the pre-production period creating looks for a large cast of principals, dancers and extras. "The trailer was wall-to-wall wigs," she said. "We kept styling them and playing with them, discovering different designs for each one as we worked."

Overall, the look for the principals was a small head, but Hatsumomo

was an exception. "I made her wig really, really high," said Quiyou. "The higher it got, the better it looked, which is actually closer to the traditional style. The extras also had a more traditional look."

Finding the right look for Sayuri's solo dance scene was another challenge. "I had been creating gigantic hairdos with big ornaments," Quiyou recalled, "until I looked at her rehearsal and saw what she had to do. I got a really long wig, parted it down the

center, put it in a ponytail, and wrapped it in red. Then I added long pieces to make it very kabuki-looking and let it hang over her face like a curtain—really simple and quite beautiful."

A real-life *maiko* must surrender herself to the hairdresser every week or two. Each hairstyle starts with all of the hair stretched stick-straight with flattening irons and pulled into a tight ponytail. Volume and shape are added with Tibetan yak hairpieces, hairpins, lacquered wooden bands and stiff black paper hidden under the hair. Hot sticky wax keeps every hair in place and subdues potential frizz all the way to the hairline. "It's better than hairspray," noted Quiyou.

A *maiko* sleeps on a special pillow designed to keep her hairdo intact. She cannot dismantle or wash her hair between visits to the hairdresser. A common side effect of the years of yanking and waxing is a permanent round bald spot on the crown—the mark of a *maiko*. 🀫

133

Of all the performing arts a geisha embraces, none distinguishes her like dance. All apprentices must study the ancient art, but only a few are chosen to make it their specialty.

"Dance is the ultimate form of artistic expression in the geisha world," said Rob Marshall, "and so it has a very special place in our film. It was incredibly exciting for us to blend our vision as artists with the beautiful traditions of Japanese dance in telling Sayuri's story."

John DeLuca, Marshall's supervising choreographer on *Chicago*, headed the *Memoirs of a Geisha* dance team. Denise Faye, also a *Chicago* veteran, was DeLuca's associate choreographer, and Miyako Tachibana, a teacher at the 67-year-old Fujima Kansuma School

in Los Angeles, was the Japanese dance consultant. Her mother, the school's founder and artistic director, lent moral support as well as expertise to the production.

The collaboration produced a unique hybrid, modern and new. "Japanese dance is very controlled and often slow, based primarily on *plié* (bending from the knees) and subtle, refined movements," said Tachibana. "Rob and John and Denise absorbed our fundamentals, then added their own Hollywood razzle-dazzle. It is magical."

DeLuca saw geisha as kindred spirits to New York City Ballet ballerinas. "They are a certain physical type and they train, train, train," he said. But the style of movement is very different. Geisha dance with their knees together and toes in. As a Bob Fosse dancer early in his career, DeLuca long ago mastered "turn-in," in addition to traditional ballet turn-out, but there was much more to learn about Japanese dance.

DeLuca spent most of a year researching its themes and history. He and Marshall attended the 103-year-old Spring Festival dances, or *Miyako Odori*, in Kyoto's Gion *hanamachi*. They also saw legendary Kabuki actor/dancer Tamasaburo

Banda perform in Japan. "He is a god to us now," said DeLuca.

DeLuca also collected images that excited him, and noticed that a picture of eight-inch platform sandals drew strong reactions whenever he showed it to anyone.

OPPOSITE: Choreographer John DeLuca and Youki Kudoh on the spring maiko dance set (Belasco Theatre, Los Angeles). RIGHT: DeLuca in rehearsal.

Choreography
Being the Music

"People always commented on the shoes and the way you walk in them—toes in," he recalled.

The black lacquered shoes, which courtesans wore to lead parades in ancient festivals, became DeLuca's starting point for Sayuri's solo. He had the costume department make him, Faye and Tachibana each a pair, but before setting a single step, he created a scenario. "A choreographer has to be a writer first. You need that springboard to excite your actor."

In his scenario, a grieving courtesan, abandoned by her lover, has decided to kill herself, a familiar theme in Japanese dance. She slips into the shoes and starts down a narrow path where blinding snow envelops her. The wind takes her cape. She loses her shoes, and then her parasol. She looks back, hoping he might be coming for her, but sees only memories. The path ahead brings madness and death.

DeLuca began choreographing the solo before he met Ziyi Zhang,

a trained dancer. "The first part of the dance I taught her was the shoes, and she jumped right on them," he said. "She was fearless. I would have had to throw that all away if she hadn't been!"

She danced on a narrow runway, or *hanamichi* (not *hanamachi*, which means geisha district), making the solo more Kabuki-like. "That was Rob's idea," said DeLuca. "The narrowness made it even more difficult with the lights and the snow."

Zhang agreed. "It was definitely a challenge, and I ended up swallowing huge mouthfuls of fake snow. When I first saw the shoes, I thought they were props. Then John told me I had to dance in them!

"The dance involved a high degree of acting," she said. "The music was very moving and very much suited the mood of the jilted woman."

Zhang's commitment endeared her to Marshall. "I wonder if anything is too difficult for Ziyi," he said.

Tachibana felt the same way.

"I'll bet she could tap dance in those shoes if she wanted to. Being graceful in them, making it look effortless, having the kimono flow and the parasol fall into place is a lot to think about. She handled it magnificently."

DeLuca and Tachibana danced the solo themselves when the camera was rehearsing the moves. "All you can do is practice, practice, practice with those shoes," said Tachibana, who was jittery her first time down the *hanamichi*. "With the snow, the darkness and the music, it was like being transported to another time and place."

Marshall and DeLuca always believed the film's key roles called for actresses with dance backgrounds and cast another former dancer, Michelle Yeoh, as Mameha. "She and Ziyi both have

Opposite: John DeLuca works on Sayuri's solo. Right: Ziyi Zhang rehearses the solo with DeLuca.

natural movement," said Faye. "They were fast at picking up the right things, the head and hand movements."

Yeoh understood that less was more with Mameha. "Her movements are very contained. She is the epitome of geisha, so everything must look effortless," Yeoh explained. "As a dancer and athlete, I learned the discipline of being very focused and observant, which is the Japanese way of learning anything."

Gong Li was a wizard with her fans, the foremost prop in Japanese dance. Her *coup de grâce*, nicknamed the "DeLuca Fan Flip," was designed to put Sayuri in her place one night at the teahouse. DeLuca created three flips of increasing difficulty. "The third one was so hard I never expected her to get it, but she did, and even embellished it."

She began with a jaunty *kaname gaeshi*, twirling a single fan on her fingers. Then Pumpkin, played by

Youki Kudoh, handed her a second fan. Li swung them both like pendulums, released them in the air, let them spin one complete revolution, and finally caught one in each hand.

DeLuca decided to make a statement with fans in the spring-themed *maiko* dance, which precedes Sayuri's winter solo (festival programs typically highlight the seasons). "To me, what is unbelievably beautiful about a fan is the way it moves through space, like it's taking flight," he said. "I thought about mixing huge fans with small ones, and making the big ones see-through."

Before they begin to move, the 10 *maiko* onstage, five with

OPPOSITE: Associate choreographer Denise Faye, John DeLuca and Rob Marshall watch a maiko *dance rehearsal scene. RIGHT: Japanese dance consultant Miyako Tachibana (right) rehearses with Youki Kudoh (center).*

traditional fans and five with fantastical ones, present a perfect springtime tableau. "When they are all in motion, and the music escalates, it is mesmerizing," said Tachibana. "That fan was a spectacle in itself."

For DeLuca, the big fan was not just a stimulating visual prop. "It was another way of communicating that we are telling Sayuri's story as a fable, rather than strictly replicating geisha culture of the 1930s."

The spring *maiko* dancers came from traditional Japanese and Hollywood-style dance backgrounds. Many of the little girls in the dance class scene were students at Fujima Kansuma in Los Angeles. "Our students are all ages. For us, developing this art is a lifetime process," said Tachibana.

Tachibana's mother provided rare Japanese dance props including *te shishi*, a small carved wooden lion's head attached to a long scarf, and a *sandangasa*, com-

posed of three large connected discs. The dancer holds one disc in each hand and wears the third on her head. "Rob was very excited about having things people had never seen before," said Tachibana.

Whatever the exotic trimmings, DeLuca has always believed that

dancers speak the same language. "Even with counting—some girls need their 'five, six, seven, eight,' and others have never counted in their lives. They just feel it. It's the same end result. You respond to the breath of it. You become the music." ▨

Sumo exhibitions began as harvest celebrations nearly 1500 years ago and evolved into entertainment for the emperor. Today, sumo is the national sport of Japan.

Mainoumi and Dewaarashi, the sumo combatants who performed in the film's sumo sequence, are both retired champions from Japan. The referee, who was Japan's top sumo referee, recently retired after 45 years in the ring.

While Dewaarashi won his career matches because of his imposing size, the diminutive Mainoumi, now a popular sumo commentator, was living proof of the sumo principle that the smaller opponent can throw his challenger off balance and use his massive size against him.

Although there are no weight classes in Japanese pro sumo, there is a height requirement and Mainoumi gained the height he needed with a silicone implant in his scalp. Because his weight hovered around 220 pounds, he typically faced much larger opponents. But Mainoumi's many wins included six of his 10 career matches against 600-pound

A dance between giants

Konishiki, the heaviest sumo wrestler of all time.

"Pound for pound, Mainoumi may be the greatest sumo wrestler ever," said Andrew Freund, the film's technical advisor on sumo. "Every single match, he was fighting someone virtually double his size."

A match usually lasts a matter of seconds and the outcome is determined by psychological as well as physical skill. "You release all of your power or *ki* in the moment of the charge. Anything can happen in that explosive moment," said Freund.

Sumo training begins early and members of a *heya*, or stable, live a communal life based on tradition and hierarchy. Among many other

LEFT: Rob Marshall and Mainoumi on the sumo set. ABOVE: Recently retired referee Shonozuke Kimura, left, appears in the film. OPPOSITE: Dewaarashi and Mainoumi perform pre-match rituals.

challenges, every pro-sumo
wrestler must be able to do a full
split, like a ballerina.

The pre-match rituals performed
today have been part of sumo for
centuries. The opponents raise
their arms before engaging to
show they have no concealed
weapons, which is also why they
are virtually naked except for a
belt called a *mawashi*.

Ceremonial clapping signifies
that the opponents are ready to
begin. They lift each leg high in the
air, then stomp it down to demon-
strate flexibility, strength and balance.
They crouch, glower and begin the
match in unison. To win, a con-
tender must shove his opponent out
of the ring, or force him to touch
the ground with any part of the body
other than the soles of the feet.

For the Japanese, sumo is more
than just a sport, it is a way of
life. "Three things matter in life:
sumo, business and war," Nobu
tells Sayuri. "Understand one
and you know them all."

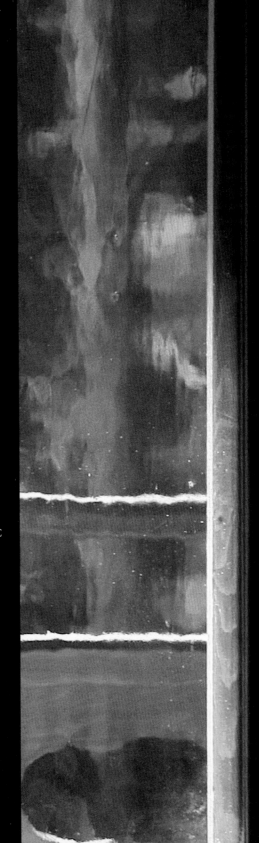

COLUMBIA PICTURES
DREAMWORKS PICTURES
SPYGLASS ENTERTAINMENT
PRESENT

AN
AMBLIN ENTERTAINMENT
DOUGLAS WICK & LUCY FISHER
PRODUCTION

A ROB MARSHALL FILM

MEMOIRS
OF A GEISHA

ZIYI ZHANG
KEN WATANABE
MICHELLE YEOH
KOJI YAKUSHO
YOUKI KUDOH
and GONG LI

Music by JOHN WILLIAMS

Costume Designer COLLEEN ATWOOD

Co-Producer JOHN DeLUCA

Editor PIETRO SCALIA, A.C.E

Production Designer JOHN MYHRE

Director of Photography DION BEEBE, ACS, ASC

Executive Producers
ROGER BIRNBAUM
GARY BARBER
PATRICIA WHITCHER
BOBBY COHEN

Based on the book by ARTHUR GOLDEN

Screenplay by
ROBIN SWICORD and DOUG WRIGHT

Produced by
LUCY FISHER
DOUGLAS WICK
STEVEN SPIELBERG

Directed by ROB MARSHALL

Acknowledgments

Acknowledgment is made by the publisher to the following for their wonderful contributions to this book:

From the production: Director Rob Marshall, co-producer/choreographer John DeLuca, executive producer Patty Whitcher, geisha consultant Liza Dalby, production designer John Myhre, costume designer Colleen Atwood, director of photography Dion Beebe, make-up designer Noriko Watanabe, hair designer Lyndell Quiyou, Japanese dance consultant Miyako Tachibana, set decorator Gretchen Rau, associate producer Leeann Stonebreaker, production manager/Japan Cellin Gluck, art director Tomas Voth, art department coordinator Lisa Vasconcellos, sumo consultant Andrew Freund, epk producer Laura Davis, the always-helpful Trevor Sagan and Michael Totten, and the utterly indispensable Arthur Roses.

From Red Wagon Entertainment: Producers Lucy Fisher and Douglas Wick, executive producer Bobby Cohen, and Meghan Snyder.

From DreamWorks Pictures and Amblin Entertainment: Producer Steven Spielberg and Marvin Levy.

From Sony Pictures Entertainment: Amy Pascal, Geoffrey Ammer, Ileen Reich, Anne Marie McDermott, George Leon, Juli Boylan, Greg Economos, Laetitia May, Grace Ressler, Cindy Irwin, and, in Japan, Kay Aoki and Jun Ogawa.

From Spyglass Entertainment: Executive producers Gary Barber and Roger Birnbaum; Karen Sortito and Susan Hua.

A special thanks to Rob Marshall and novelist Arthur Golden for their introductions, photographer David James, and writer Peggy Mulloy.

From Newmarket Press: Project editor Linda Sunshine, Timothy Shaner and Christopher Measom at Night and Day Design, and the dedicated editorial and production team.